OTHER BOOKS BY HELEN EXLEY:

Over 50's Jokes	**Cat Jokes**
Over 60's Jokes	**Golf Jokes**
Over 80's Jokes	**Life! And other disasters... 365**
Senior Moments 365	**Dog Quotes**

EDITED BY HELEN EXLEY

Published in 2019, 2023 by Helen Exley ®LONDON in Great Britain.
Design, selection and arrangement © Helen Exley Creative Ltd 2019, 2023.
All the words by Pam Brown, Odile Dormeuil, Stuart & Linda Macfarlane,
Stuart Macfarlane, Linda Macfarlane, Charlotte Gray, Helen Thomson,
Mathilde & Sébastien Forestier, Pamela Dugdale, Linda Gibson, Peter Gray,
Helen Exley, Brian Clyde and copyright © Helen Exley Creative Ltd 2019,
2023. Cartoons copyright © Bill Stott 2019, 2023. The moral rights of the
authors have been asserted.

12   11   10   9   8   7   6   5   4   3   2   1

ISBN: 978-1-78485-235-1

Helen Exley ® LONDON,
16 Chalk Hill, Watford, Herts WD19 4BG, UK
www.helenexley.com

Over 70's Jokes

CARTOONS BY BILL STOTT

Helen Exley

Seventy is...
When you get the opportunity
to get it wrong all over again.
When the only threshold you pass
is your level of boredom.
Twice the cost with only half the energy.
A veiled excuse to use your spouse
as a caddie for two weeks.
When the supermarket trolley
rattles less than your dentures.
A fashion accessory
is a shopping trolley.
Having to iron your face every morning
as the anti-wrinkle cream
no longer works.

JON NEWBOLD

Life is like
a roll of toilet paper.
The closer you get
to the end,
the faster it goes.

AUTHOR UNKNOWN

The old believe everything,
the middle-aged suspect everything,
the young know everything.

OSCAR WILDE

All diseases run int

Old people are fond
of giving good advice;
it consoles them for no longer
being capable
of setting a bad example.

FRANÇOIS DE LA ROCHEFOUCAULD

ne, old age.

RALPH WALDO EMERSON

When you are on first name terms
with your doctors, you are old.

PAM BROWN

Major Stress-Inducing Phrases

1. "Hi, Grandpa."
2. "Can I carry that for you?"
3. "I'm sure you and your daughter will like this room."
4. "May I show you something more, uh conservative?"
5. "I'm sorry, Sir, but according to this tape measure you're a size larger than that."
6. "Keep running… go for it… you can make it, Pop."
7. "You're probably looking for bonds with a shorter maturity."
8. "Sorry, Sir. This prescription has been filled twenty-seven times and was originally issued for a temporary disorder."

FRED SHOENBERG

The four stages
in accepting old age;
denial,
anger,
despair,
having a
bloody good time.

STUART & LINDA MACFARLANE

The biggest myth is that as you grow older, you gradually lose your interest in sex. This myth probably got started because younger people seem to want to have sex with each other at every available opportunity including traffic lights, whereas older people are more likely to reserve their sexual activities for special occasions such as the installation of a new Pope.

DAVE BARRY

When in his seventies
Sir Malcolm Sargent was asked
to what he attributed his great age.
"Well," he said,
"I suppose I must attribute it to
the fact that I haven't died yet."

AUTHOR UNKNOWN

I was at that time of life
when we become aware of
our plumbing, when we wake
in the night to sounds of protest
from within – joints creaking,
intestines in a riot.

PAUL BAILEY

My doctor recently told me
that jogging could add
years to my life.
I think he was right.
I feel ten years older already.

MILTON BERLE

At seventy...
you finally know all
the answers.
Trouble is
nobody asks.

MATHILDE & SÉBASTIEN FORESTIER

When I was younger
I only had one full set of teeth –
but now I've got two.
One in this glass
and the other as a mould
in the dentist's surgery.

MIKE KNOWLES

Old age
is a sort of auction game –
a rivalry between
acquaintances.
Your ten pills
against my twelve.
Twenty pills
against a pacemaker.
A pacemaker
against a hip replacement.

CHARLOTTE GRAY

Age is when
sex takes
too much planning
to be fun.

PAM BROWN

Seventy is when you
pull yourself up in the way
that once made you look like
a fashion model –
and nothing happens at all.

PAMELA DUGDALE

The secret to enjoying old age
is to appear so decrepit
that you are never asked
to do anything but to remain
healthy enough to play golf,
ski and run marathons.

MATHILDE & SÉBASTIEN FORESTIER

Geriatric Chat-Up Line
•Your place or mine –
I need a nap.

STUART & LINDA MACFARLANE

Time and trouble
will tame an advanced
young woman,
but an advanced
old woman is
uncontrollable by any
earthly force.

DOROTHY L. SAYERS

Old age is that period
when someone is too old
to take advice
but young enough to give it.

E. C. MCKENZIE

Remember – all the awful things
that happen to you when you are young
give you the intelligence never to let
them happen again. Of course,
as you get older you'll simply experience
a whole new range of disasters.
But by the time you're seventy
you'll be pretty good at dodging
all catastrophes.
And then you'll fall down the stairs.

PAM BROWN

Old age is when you have bunions on your bunions.

STUART & LINDA MACFARLANE

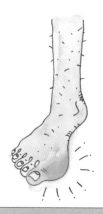

I don't need you to remind me
of my age,
I have a bladder to do that for me.

STEPHEN FRY

When you're seventy,
if your lumbago isn't acting up
and your bones aren't aching –
you're under a general anaesthetic.

LINDA GIBSON

Age is full of interest –
wondering which faculty
will desert one next.

CHARLOTTE GRAY

Gray hair usually comes along about twenty years after you thought it would make you look distinguished.

E. C. MCKENZIE

Old age is when a pretty girl
catches your eye across
a crowded train;
and as you think of romance,
she offers you her seat.

STUART MACFARLANE

Dear Diary:
I am very disappointed
for I did not receive a single
Valentine card today.
Which is very surprising
for I am sure
that I sent myself two.

LINDA GIBSON

I wouldn't say her face
was showing its age,
but last week she was
followed home by a group
of archaeologists.

MIKE KNOWLES

The terrible truth
is that immediately after
buying a replacement you will find
the item you had lost.

STUART & LINDA MACFARLANE

A stockbroker urged me
to buy a stock that would triple
its value every year.
I told him,
"At my age, I don't even buy
green bananas."

CLAUDE PEPPER

Youth is a wonderful thing;
what a crime
to waste it on children.

GEORGE BERNARD SHAW

Old is the time of life when even your birthday suit needs pressing.

BOB HOPE

An old woman's talking to her husband sentimentally about their courtship. "Ah, do you remember how you used to nibble my ear?" "Yes." "You never do it nowadays." "No. Well, by the time I've found my teeth, the urge has gone."

AUTHOR UNKNOWN

Small boy:
"Grandfather, were you in the Ark?"
Grandfather (very grumpy):
"No, I was not in the Ark."
Small boy (with relentless logic):
"Well, why weren't you
drowned then?"

SIR ANTONY PART

It's old age when each day makes you feel two days older.

E. C. MCKENZIE

The police didn't believe me when I explained that I was driving fast so that I could reach my destination before I forgot where I was going.

STUART & LINDA MACFARLANE

After seventy, you still chase women, but only downhill.

BOB HOPE

Nowadays there's a pill
for everything – to keep your nose
from running, to keep you regular,
to keep your heart beating,
to keep your hair from falling out,
to improve your muscle tone…
Why, thanks to advances
in medical science,
every day people are dying
who never looked better.

AUTHOR UNKNOWN

Old age begins with
the sudden realisation
that your children
are older than you
imagine yourself to be.

STUART & LINDA MACFARLANE

Don't talk to me about
Valentine's Day.
At my age an affair of the heart
is a bypass operation.

JOAN RIVERS

You know you're
growing old when...
You still have
the old spark,
but it takes more
puffing to ignite.

RICHARD LEDERER

An old chap in his seventies
was concerned about the lack of
his sex drive and consulted his doctor.
"Well, what would you expect
at your age?" said the medic.
The old geezer was still worried,
"But my next door neighbour
is over eighty and he says he gets
it every night."
The doc thought for a moment.
"Well, why don't you say it too?"

GEORGE COOTE

I can't wait to tell
my grandkids
I was born before the Internet.

AUTHOR UNKNOWN

Why does my compute

Today I joined
the hashtag revolution.
#IAMNOTTOOOLDTOBECOOL

STUART & LINDA MACFARLANE

hate me so much?

PETER GRAY

These days even though
I use my own name
as my email password,
I will forget it every time
I try to log in.

STUART MACFARLANE

Old age
isn't so bad
when you consider
the alternative.

MAURICE CHEVALIER

Inflation is when you pay
fifteen dollars for the ten-dollar haircut
you used to get for five dollars
when you had hair.

SAM EWING

In youth
we run into
difficulties;
in old age
difficulties
run into us.

JOSH BILLINGS

Every time I try to
take out a new lease on life,
the landlord raises the rent.

ASHLEIGH BRILLIANT

Perhaps one has
to be very old
before one learns
how to
be amused rather
than shocked.

PEARL S. BUCK

Age is mind
over matter.
As long as you
don't mind,
it don't matter.

MUHAMMAD ALI

The best part of being old
is that you no longer
need to set your children
a good example.

MATHILDE & SÉBASTIEN FORESTIER

The worst thing
about Old Age
is the speeding up of time…
I had a party for my fiftieth
birthday and another
for my sixtieth,
three or four years later.

RAYMOND BRIGGS

A woman knows she's getting old
when she wears everything for comfort.

PAM BROWN

When you're young,
you want to be master of your fate
and captain of your soul.
When you're older,
you'll settle for being master
of your weight
and captain of your bowling team.

GEORGE ROBERTS

Middle age
is when the best
exercise is one of
discretion.

DR. LAURENCE J. PETER

…there are three signs of ageing.
The first is that you tend
to forget things rather easily –
and for the life of me,
I don't know what
the other two things are.

EMANUEL CELLER

The secret of staying young
is to live honestly,
eat slowly, sleep sufficiently,
work industriously,
worship faithfully... and then...
lie about your age.

LUCILLE BALL

The happiest time of life
is between seventy and eighty,
and I advise everyone
to hurry up and get there
as soon as possible.

JOSEPH CHOATE

How is it that our memory
is good enough to retain
the least triviality that happens to us,
and yet not good enough
to recollect how often we have told it
to the same person?

FRANÇOIS DE LA ROCHEFOUCAULD

Old Fred fronted up to the Sperm Bank
and insisted on making a donation.
The matron looked at him doubtfully.
He was 83. But Fred would not be
denied and protested that he was as fit
as a prize bull. Finally she gave Fred
a little jar, ushered him towards
a cubicle and closed the door.
For the next few minutes all she
could hear was much grunting and puffing
and it went on for so long she got worried.
She knocked on the door.
"Are you okay?" she called.
"No. I need help," said Fred.
"I can't get the lid off this bloody jar."

GEORGE COOTE

Old age? That's the period
of life when you buy
a see-through nightgown
and then remember
you don't know anybody
who can still
see through one.

BETTE DAVIS

When I was young
I thought that money
was the most important thing
in life; now that I am old
I know that it is.

OSCAR WILDE

Seventy! Now is the time
to make your mark on the world –
explore the Antarctic
or become an astronaut.
Make your mind up to
take on exciting new challenges –
straight after your afternoon nap.

AUTHOR UNKNOWN

If you don't have wrinkles, you haven't laughed enough.

PHYLLIS DILLER

One does not feel old
until one sees oneself unexpectedly
in a plate glass window.

PAMELA DUGDALE

My doctor
said I look like
a million dollars –
green and
wrinkled.

RED SKELTON

The saddest part
of birthdays,
there really is no doubt,
is each year I've more
candles and less breath
to blow them out.

DONNA EVLETH

Youth would be an ideal state if it came a little later in life.

LORD HERBERT ASQUITH

Childishness follows us all
the days of our life.
If anybody seems wise
it is only because his follies
are in keeping with his age
and circumstances.

FRANCOIS, DUC DE LA ROCHEFOUCAULD

One night I was so confused
that I got into the bath
without taking off my clothes.
But it didn't matter
because I'd also forgotten
to turn on the tap.

AUTHOR UNKNOWN

Oldies like to think of themselves
as curmudgeons.
Only a misguided few
are incessantly cheerful,
and those people
must be avoided at all costs.

NIELA ELIASON

Geriatric Chat-Up Line
• My pacemaker fluttered when I saw you.

STUART & LINDA MACFARLANE

At about seventy
you still get 'the urge' –
but can't
remember what for…

AUTHOR UNKNOWN

WHAT ABOUT THE BODY JUNK?
The scars, the wrinkles,
the stretchmarks, liver spots, polyps,
the hopeless meaningless flab,
the wonky tortoiseshell toe-nails
and bags under the eyes
like SCROTAL SACS,
the weird bruises old ladies get,
the furrowed brow
and no sign of a neck at all?
And that was just on the OUTSIDE…

LUCY ELLMANN

There's no need
to feel miserable on your
seventieth birthday –
there are two decades
ahead for that.

LINDA GIBSON

Being young is beautiful, bu

eing old is comfortable.

MARIE VON EBNER ESCHENBACH

You're past it...
when you look forward
to a dull evening in.

PAM BROWN

Now that I'm
over sixty,
I'm veering toward
respectability.

SHELLEY WINTERS

Doctor: "I don't know quite how to put this – but your heart is on its last legs and you've only got six months to live."

"Is there nothing I can do?" asked the shocked man.

"Well," said the doctor, "you can give up alcohol and cut out smoking. Don't eat any fried food or sugar and don't even think about sex."

"And this will make me live longer?" the man asked hopefully.

"No," replied the doctor, "it'll just seem like longer."

AUTHOR UNKNOWN

One of the best parts
of growing older?
You can flirt all you like
since you've become harmless.

LIZ SMITH

Sex after ninety is like
trying to shoot pool with a rope.
Even putting my cigar
in its holder is a thrill.

GEORGE BURNS

At my age,
when a girl flirts
with me in
the movies, she's after
my popcorn.

MILTON BERLE

As a young man,
I used to have four supple members
and one stiff one.
Now I have four stiff and one supple.

HENRI DUC D'AUMALE

Age does not automatically
make one loveable.
If you were a pig at twenty,
you're likely to be
even piggier at seventy five.

PAM BROWN

Advantages of being an Oldie...
You don't need to worry about
getting your beauty sleep.
You can win national moaning
competitions. You can impress members
of the opposite sex
with all your operation scars.
You can now afford to do all the things
you are no longer able to do.
Hair maintenance involves sending it out
to the dry cleaners once a month.
You have become an expert on TV soaps.

MATHILDE & SÉBASTIEN FORESTIER

I taught my cat, Elsie, to remind me when it's her feeding time. Poor Elsie is getting as forgetful as me. She seems to be reminding me eight times a day. It's costing me a fortune!

STUART & LINDA MACFARLANE

I've been given so many
spare body parts that I've just been
presented with an award for recycling.

LINDA GIBSON

Middle age is that span in life
when you admit to no longer being
young and deny being old.

FRED SHOENBERG

Nothing ages a man faster
than trying to prove
he's still as young as ever.

E. C. MCKENZIE

Age. That period of life
in which we compound
for the vices that remain
by reviling those
we have no longer
the vigour to commit.

AMBROSE BIERCE

We grow with years more
fragile in body, but morally stouter,
and can throw off the chill of
a bad conscience almost at once.

LOGAN PEARSALL SMITH

Young men want to be faithful
and are not,
old men want to be faithless and cannot.

OSCAR WILDE

You're never too old to act
like a love-crazed teenager.

MATHILDE & SÉBASTIEN FORESTIER

I am always finding new ways
of avoiding senior moments.
I keep a pair of spectacles in
every room of the house
and my address written on my
door key – If I could only remember
which house is mine
I could get a pair of spectacles
and then be able to read
the address on my keyring.

LINDA GIBSON

In a survey for Modern
Maturity magazine,
men over seventy-five said
they had sex once a week.
Which proves that
some old guys
lie about sex too.

IRV GILMAN

You're still young
if the morning after the night before
still makes the night before
worth the morning after.

BOB GODDARD

You're never too old

to become younger.

MAE WEST

Inside every older woman
is a young girl wondering
what the hell happened.

CORA HARVEY ARMSTRONG

Avoid mirrors.
So long as
you dodge them
you are slim,
clear-skinned,
wide-eyed and
very beautiful.

PAMELA DUGDALE

Age does not wither
your emotions, even if your
derrière slumps southward.

CHERRI GILMAN

She could very well
pass for forty-three, in the dusk
with a light behind her.

W. S. GILBERT

It's hard to impress people
with your body's disasters when you
can't remember the list!

HELEN EXLEY

A woman is neve

Make-up in old age
has the trick of congealing
in every wrinkle.
Better to look ordinarily old than
the spitting image of Medusa.

CHARLOTTE GRAY

At seventy...
a wild night is
going to bed at eight
with a cup of cocoa.

STUART & LINDA MACFARLANE

oo old to yearn.

GRAFFITI

Last night I spent
several hours
searching
for my phone.
No luck –
but at least
I know where
the remote control,
kettle and microwave
disappeared to.

STUART & LINDA MACFARLANE

Now that I'm retired I feel
obliged to take up knitting
and make everyone garish sweaters
that are far too big.

LINDA GIBSON

You may not be able to muster
a thirty-two *fouettes* any more...
but you can still do a soft shoe shuffle
when you're seventy-five.

PAM BROWN

Some of our modern grandmothers
are so young and spry
they help the Boy Scouts across
the street.

E. C. MCKENZIE

Last night a lady
came to my house
collecting money for a charity
that helps the aged.
I gave her some money –
she gave it straight back to me.

STUART & LINDA MACFARLANE

Another good thing about
being poor is that when you are
seventy your children will not have you
declared legally insane in order
to gain control of your estate.

WOODY ALLEN

Don't smoke too much,
drink too much,
eat too much
or work too much.
We're all on the road to the grave –
but there's no reason to be
in the passing lane.

ROBERT ORBEN

You're getting along in years
when the only urge you feel
in the spring is to climb
out of your long underwear.

E. C. MCKENZIE

Whenever a man's friends
begin to compliment him
about looking young,
he may be sure that they think
his is growing old.

WASHINGTON IRVING

I wake up in the morning,
and it takes me a half-hour
to find my glasses,
just so I can look for my teeth,
to tell my wife
to find my hair.

RICHARD JENNI

The older the fiddle, the sweeter the tune.

ENGLISH PROVERB

When you finally learn how to do it, you're too old for the good parts.

RUTH GORDON

I do wish I could tell you my age, but it is impossible. It keeps changing all the time.

GREER GARSON

What a wretched lot of old shrivelled
creatures we shall be by-and-by.
Never mind – the uglier we get
in the eyes of others, the lovelier
we shall be to each other.

GEORGE ELIOT (MARY ANN EVANS)

I have had so many
body parts replaced
my wife has taken
to calling me
her million dollar man.

BRIAN CLYDE

By the time you reach
75 years of age
you've learnt everything.
All you have to do is to try
and remember it.

GEORGE COOTE

The first half of life
consists of the capacity to enjoy
without the chance,
the last half consists of the chance
without capacity.

MARK TWAIN

Oh, the bitter sweet irony of it all.
As a youngster I desperately
wanted a really fast sports car
but could never afford one.
Now I regularly get to dash across town
in a high speed ambulance.

STUART & LINDA MACFARLANE

Seventy is just forty

We women will never admit
to being in our 70's, 40, yes 50?...
well, maybe. But 70? Never!
Once she reaches this age
the most respectable woman
will turn into blatant liar.
Me, 70? Never! I'm 45 if I'm a day.

MIKE KNOWLES

He used to buy her lacy negligees.
She used to buy him jaunty turtlenecks.
But now they've moved
into another phase.
More osteoporosis and less sex.

JUDITH VIORST

with attitude.

STUART & LINDA MACFARLANE

…you're at
the dangerous age
and nobody is offering
you any danger.

MARTIN A RAGAWAY

On my seventieth birthday
I went to this Harley Street
    plastic surgeon.
The top man in his field.
I said, "Look here!
Can you give me the face and body
    of Kim Kardashian?"
He took one look at me
and replied, "Madam!
If I could do that I'd be raising
the dead and walking on water."

MIKE KNOWLES

Your seventies is the stage in your life
when you become mature,
reliable and dependable.
Or, as your grandchildren put it,
boring, predictable and irritating.

LINDA MACFARLANE

Do not resist growing old – Many are denied the privilege!

ART LINKLETTER

The old have
a mental map
in their heads
of loos
with easy access.

PAM BROWN

"How old are you?" asked
the little boy. "Very, very old," I replied.
"Fifty?" quizzed the young lad.
"Best think very, very, very, very old,"
I said softly.

STUART MACFARLANE

You can't turn back the clock. But you can wind it up again.

BONNIE PRUDDEN

Respect old people.
They graduated school without
Google or Wikipedia.

AUTHOR UNKNOWN

I wouldn't say she was wrinkled,
but last year she went on holiday to India.
And when she was sunbathing
next to this river one of the local women
used her face as a washboard.

MIKE KNOWLES

In mathematical terms old age
is a condition reached
when the rate of your receding hairline
is directly proportional
to the expansion of your waist.

ANGUS WALKER

I would drink
and dance
and flirt all night –
if I could only
stay awake.

ODILE DORMEUIL

Having taken my situation
into account I have regrettably
had to re-evaluate
and make some changes.
Now, instead of wanting to
become an astronaut
I have decided to take up ballet.

LINDA GIBSON

You're past it…
when the spirit's willing
but the flesh is
too flipping tired.

CHARLOTTE GRAY

THE POSITIVE SIDE

You can embarrass your family
by entering glamorous granny
or good-looking grandfather
competitions.
You don't need to be polite anymore –
people expect you to be critical,
rude and cantankerous.
You can talk incessantly about
the good old days.
Your failing eyesight saves you
the anguish of seeing your
disintegrating body.

MATHILDE & SÉBASTIEN FORESTIER

You know you're growing old
when the best part of the day
is over when your alarm clock goes off;
you and your teeth don't sleep together;
you feel that it's the morning after,
when you haven't gone out
the night before.

RICHARD LEDERER

My dating site age: 59
My legal age: 73
The age I feel: 94
The age I act: 11

LINDA GIBSON

My wife teases me
that I tell the same joke every time
we meet up with our friends.
Oh yeah! Well, how can that be
for they find it so hilarious every time?

BRIAN CLYDE

Middle age is when you go to bed
at night and hope you feel better
in the morning.
Old age is when you go to bed
at night and hope
you wake up in the morning.

GROUCHO MARX

One of the privileges
of old age is to relate
experiences that nobody
will believe
and give advice
that nobody will follow.

E. C. MCKENZIE

Age only matters
when one is ageing.
Now that I have arrived
at a great age,
I might just as well be twenty.

PABLO PICASSO

The young
have aspirations that never
come to pass,
the old have reminiscences
of what never happened.

SAKI

Old is understanding Cat talk
better than Computer jargon.

PAM BROWN

The secret is to becom

A new broom sweeps clean,
but an old one knows the corners.

ENGLISH SAYING

You know you're getting old
when little old ladies
help you across the road.

MATHILDE & SÉBASTIEN FORESTIER

I'm so old that bartenders
check my pulse instead of my I.D.

LOUISE BOWIE

vise before you get old.

AUTHOR UNKNOWN

From birth to age eighteen,
a girl needs good parents;
from eighteen to thirty-five
she needs good looks;
from thirty-five to fifty-five
she needs a good personality;
and from fifty-five on
she needs cash.

SOPHIE TUCKER

My husband got very upset because I forgot his birthday. Truth is I didn't forget his birthday – I forgot I was married!

LINDA MACFARLANE

My grandchildren were giggling
and laughing with delight
for they thought I was doing
an impersonation of a frog.
Sadly I now make
that croaking sound every time
I kneel down or get up again.

STUART & LINDA MACFARLANE

The only two things
we do with greater frequency
in middle age are
urinate and attend funerals.

FRED SHOENBERG

About the only thing that comes to us without effort is old age.

GLORIA PITZER

I intend
to spend
my old age
being
outrageous.

STUART MACFARLANE

I keep a notepad with me
at all times and write in it
all the things
that I must remember.
The most important thing
I must remember
is emblazoned in block capitals
on the front:
WRITE DOWN
THE THINGS
YOU MUST REMEMBER.

LINDA GIBSON

I read that eating a large
portion of broccoli
every day helps to improve
memory. I've decided
that having a bad memory
isn't so bad after all.

STUART & LINDA MACFARLANE

You know you're old
when you choose your cereal
for the fiber,
not the toy.

RICHARD LEDERER

By the time
a man is wise enough
to watch his step,
he's too old
to go anywhere.

BILLY CRYSTAL

Last night I had a typical cholesterol-free dinner: baked squash, skimmed milk, and gelatin. I'm sure this will not make me live any longer, but I know it's going to seem longer.

GROUCHO MARX

Today I made three new friends.
Well to be more precise
I suddenly remembered
the names of three friends
I had completely forgotten about!

AMANDA BELL

"Are you going to have candles
on your birthday cake?"
"No, it's a birthday party,
not a torchlight procession."

CINDY PATTERSON

I saw Romeo and Juliet today
for the fifth time this week.
Wow – that's a shocking ending –
I didn't see that coming.

STUART & LINDA MACFARLANE

Love is like
the measles.
All the worse
when it comes
late in life.

DOUGLAS JERROLD

When grace is joined with wrinkles,
it is wonderful.
There is an unspeakable dawn
in happy old age.

VICTOR HUGO

Old friends like to share interests:
art, cinema, gardens, cars,
arthritis,
rheumatism,
angina,
indigestion.

PAM BROWN

Three elderly men discussing
death and the afterlife
were telling each other how they
would like to leave this life, as follows:-
1st old man:
"I would like to die climbing Everest
after planting a flag on the summit."
2nd old man:
"I would like to die bowling the last ball
down in a vital test match."
3rd old man:
"I would like to die in bed,
shot by a jealous husband."

LORD AYLESTONE

He told me the wrinkles
on his face were
laughter lines but nothing
is that funny.

GEORGE MELLY

Never forget –
the reflection in the shop window
isn't you. It's a trick of the light.

ODILE DORMEUIL

Age is a marvellous disguise.
You can creep up on officialdom
and frighten it half to death.

PAM BROWN

Old age is when a guy
keeps turning off lights
for economical
rather than
romantic reasons.

PIERRE DUPONT

Old age doesn't
keep men from
chasing women;
they just have trouble
remembering why.

AUTHOR UNKNOWN

I said to my husband,
my boobs have gone,
my stomach's gone,
say something nice about
my legs. He said,
"Blue goes with everything."

JOAN RIVERS

The time to begin mos

At my age, getting a second
doctor's opinion
is like switching slot machines.

JIMMY CARTER

hings is ten years ago.

MIGNON MCLAUGHLIN

There are other fruits
I could eat for breakfast, but I prefer
prunes because they've got
more wrinkles than I have.

GEORGE BURNS

I have gold fillings in my teeth,
titanium pins in my legs
and cobalt stents in my heart.
I'm terrified to go out
in case I get melted down for
precious metal.

BRIAN CLYDE

Her birthday cake
had so many candles on it
she was fined for air pollution.

E. C. MCKENZIE

He's so absent-minded
that he left home
without his watch,
then looked at it to see
if he had time to go back
and get it.

AUTHOR UNKNOWN

Every morning and every evening
I do fifty push-ups.
Then I sleep in a desperate effort to
build my energy reserves back up.

STUART MACFARLANE

Don't take life so seriously... it's not permanent.

KATHY HOLDER

Everyone has their folly,
but the greatest folly of all…
is not to have one.

NIKOS KAZANTZAKIS

I was reading about this footballer's wife who was suing him for divorce. She claimed the game had ruined their sex life. The judge asked her how and she said, "First we turn the bedroom into a miniature football pitch and before he'll hug and kiss me I have to score a goal."

AUTHOR UNKNOWN

Happiness
is a warm
bed pan.

CHRISTOPHER HUDSON

My diseases are asthma
and dropsy and,
what is less curable, seventy-five.

DR. SAMUEL JOHNSON

I don't do alcohol any more –
I get the same effect
just standing up fast.

AUTHOR UNKNOWN

I had a nice quiet
seventieth birthday –
I turned my hearing aid down.

MIKE KNOWLES

A man who
correctly guesses
a woman's age
may be smart,
but he's not
very bright.

LUCILLE BALL

We learn from experience
that people never learn anything
from experience.

GEORGE BERNARD SHAW

If God had to give a woman wrinkles,
He might at least have put them
on the soles of her feet.

NINON DE L'ENCLOS

The whiter my hair becomes,
the more ready people
are to believe what I say.

BERTRAND RUSSELL

Old, old friends on shopping
expeditions have legs that
give out at the same moment –
which means a co-ordinated
move to the nearest cafe.

CHARLOTTE GRAY

The best mirro

When I meet a man whose name
I cannot remember,
I give myself two minutes,
then if it is a hopeless case I always say
"And how is the old complaint?"

BENJAMIN DISRAELI

is an old friend.

GEORGE HERBERT

Wisdom doesn't automatically
come with old age.
Nothing does – except wrinkles.

ABIGAIL VAN BUREN

In youth
it is called stupidity.
In middle age,
absent-mindedness.
In old age,
Short Term
Memory Loss.

ODILE DORMEUIL

…the real problem
with retirement
is that it gives you more time
to read magazine articles
about the problems
of retirement.

MARTIN A RAGAWAY

Suddenly
there are hills
where none
used to be.

PAMELA DUGDALE

Experience:
A comb life gives you after you
lose your hair.

JUDITH STERN

You know that you're
hitting seventy when the heat
from your birthday cake candles
sets off the fire alarm.

LINDA GIBSON

Young people feel tired
after a party.
I feel exhausted for two days
before the party begins.

HELEN THOMSON

Old is when
– the reflection
in a mirror
has nothing
to do with you.

PAM BROWN

Exercise daily, eat wisely, die anyway.

AUTHOR UNKNOWN

As one slowly deteriorates
it is very comforting to have friends
who are falling apart
at the same speed.

PAMELA DUGDALE

"Think young, stay young,"
they say. Trouble is,
the method does not seem to apply
to the knees.

PETER GRAY

With mirth
and laughter
let old wrinkles come.

WILLIAM SHAKESPEARE

If the young only knew; if the old only could.

FRENCH PROVERB

Enjoy your seventies –
these are the 'good old days'
you'll extol when you are ninety.

LINDA GIBSON

At 15 you get a thrill
from riding a bicycle.
At 25 you get a thrill
from riding a Harley Davidson.
At 55 you get a thrill
from riding a fast sports car.
At 75 you get a thrill
from lying flat out on a comfy sofa.

STUART & LINDA MACFARLANE